# Why LS or EAL is the Wrong Question:

## Serving ELLs with Learning Issues
## in Inclusive Schools

## Leading The Way Collaborative Team of Authors

| | |
|---|---|
| Kelly Armitage | International School Bangkok |
| Trish Curtain | NIST International School |
| Bill Hanagan | International School of Beijing |
| Ochan Kusuma-Powell | Education Across Frontiers & Next Frontier Inclusion |
| Laura Mohl | Singapore American School |
| Jon Nordmeyer | WIDA Consortium |
| Bill Powell | Education Across Frontiers & Next Frontier Inclusion |
| Sean Powell | Next Frontier Inclusion & NYC Department of Education |
| Danette Sack | American School of The Hague |
| Cindy Warner-Dobrowski | International School Bangkok |

**First Reader**

| | |
|---|---|
| Gordon Eldridge | International School of Brussels |

**Editors**

| | |
|---|---|
| Jon Nordmeyer | WIDA Consortium |
| Kristen Pelletier | International School of Brussels |
| Danette Sack | American School of The Hague |

# Contents

## PART I: INTRODUCTION

> ### Who is Mai and what does she need?
>
> *Mai is a third grader who has been at the International School of the World (ISW) for four months. Mai is originally from Vietnam but has lived in Kenya and Spain, attending both international and local schools. Upon initial admissions screening, she passed the English as an Additional Language (EAL) screening and was determined not to require any EAL support at ISW. According to her school records, Mai was performing at grade level in all areas at her previous schools.*
>
> *Her parents have completed the home language survey, indicating that Vietnamese is the primary language used in the home. Several teachers have reported that when her father is speaking informally to Mai around the school, he uses English to speak with Mai. Her father's English level is at an intermediate level at best and her mother is often away traveling on business. On several recent Running Records, Mai's reading level was determined to be at the middle of second grade, with decoding stronger than comprehension. Mai's teacher recently met with the counselor, as he was concerned about her reading level and mentioned Mai seemed to be "lost," not understanding verbal directions.*
>
> *The counselor arranged for the Student Support Team to meet and discuss Mai. The team recognized that Mai was reading below grade level and was somewhat "language confused" and that continuing with the strong homeroom instruction in English would help and to give her time. They pointed out that according to the admissions EAL screening, Mai did not qualify for EAL services, and her reading levels would most likely catch up. They concluded that the homeroom teacher needed to differentiate more. They determined that Mai did not qualify for Learning Support, as she was not reading one full grade level behind. Mai needed to be grouped in a flexible reading group in the homeroom, to get support with reading strategies.*
>
> *Mai currently continues to struggle and the gap is widening. The homeroom teacher is becoming more concerned and frustrated, as Mai is withdrawing and demonstrating a lack of motivation. The teacher is often overheard saying, "If only we could figure out if this was a Learning Support issue or an English Language issue, then we could help Mai be successful."*

## Re-Imagining the Issue

There is an old adage that suggests that if the only tool that we have available is a hammer, every problem will appear to be a nail. There is an inconvenient but commonplace truth embedded here that relates directly to how we address the issue of children who are in the process of learning English and who may have learning differences. We tend to see these children not as they are but through lenses that we have constructed, often using unexamined assumptions and mental models. As the story of Mai illustrates, this approach often does not serve students well.

As professionals with specialized areas of expertise, we can inadvertently slip into perceiving children through the lens of our individual professional perspectives if we are not careful. We may construct these perceptions based less on their actual learning profiles than on our own frame of reference and the structural constraints of our schools. This is not to conflate or devalue the important expertise that EAL and Learning Support specialists bring to schools, but simply to underscore that some students will greatly benefit from *both* perspectives.

---

**Whose needs do we serve?**

*Ahmed entered school in the second grade, monolingual in Arabic. He was placed in a segregated EAL class. He made little progress in learning English and in the fifth grade was referred for special needs assessment. At the end of the fifth grade, the Learning Support department referred Ahmed back to the EAL department stating that the young man did not have enough English to be accurately assessed for a learning difference. Ahmed had become a ping pong ball in an adult structured educational world that was meeting its own needs and for the most part, ignoring his.*

*Fang Wou, a charming Chinese student, who after 12 years of EAL support has only mastered social language and struggles with concept development and higher-level thinking in both Mandarin and English. Fang Wou has used her very considerable interpersonal intelligence to mask her problematic progress in developing academic language in English. The EAL department genuinely likes and cares for Fang Wou and is loath to see her stigmatized by special needs labeling.*

---

When we look at students in international schools we can expect there to be both a population of students who are engaged in learning English and a population of students who have learning differences. We can also <u>expect</u> to find a population that has characteristics of both: children who are simultaneously learning English *and* struggling with learning. This is why "LS <u>or</u> EAL?" is the wrong question. We need to adjust our thinking to consider Learning Support <u>and</u> EAL for some learners.

**Through the Looking Glass of International Schools** (We are still who we were)
Many of the structures and organizing features of international schools have developed over time in an ad hoc fashion, so no longer make sense nor serve the best interests of our students. This has implications for programs serving both English language learners and students with learning differences. Prior to World War Two, so-called "overseas" schools were basically transplanted national system schools. There were British schools, French schools, and American missionary schools. For the most part these were culturally homogeneous institutions that expected students to speak English and then learn in a rather traditional one-size-fits-all fashion.

Following World War Two as decolonization swept the developing world, we saw the emergence of "international schools". These were modeled on the previous "overseas school model" and in the early days many of these schools did not accept students who were not fluent in English or who had learning differences. However, globalization and the economic migration of families created demographic shifts in international school populations. These factors coupled with more inclusive legislation in the western anglophone countries, caused schools to address these previously excluded populations.

So in an effort to meet the educational needs of the community, international schools added EAL departments and Learning Support personnel that often functioned independently and with considerable autonomy. These were typically considered specialized areas that were added onto the mainstream classroom instruction. As a result, there was often only minimal communication and little collaborative reflection. These discrete departments encouraged "silo thinking" in which there is only one label we can apply, naturally leading to the false dichotomy: "Is this student EAL <u>or</u> LS?" This unnecessary choice put the needs of the child as secondary to the needs of the adult-imposed structures.

## Ineffective Practices and Better Practices

This list might have been seen as "best practices" at a certain time and in another context. Current research and changing practice suggest these approaches are no longer effective in supporting culturally and linguistically diverse learners in inclusive international schools:

| Ineffective Past Practices | Better Practices |
| --- | --- |
| *In order to facilitate English language learning, not allowing students to speak in L1 (the student's first language or home language) at school .* | L1 languages are linked to family communication, life, identity, and thinking. L1 languages should be embraced, appreciated, and supported as they enhance the richness of inclusive environments. |
| *Waiting until students are "proficient enough" in English before attempting to assess their learning needs.* | Tasks involving memory, attention, processing, sensory needs (to name a few cognitive processes) are more highly challenged when students are immersed in a new language. Recognize and support these processes while students are acquiring English. |
| *Interpreting standardized tests/assessments without considering what English language needs the student might have.* | Always interpret data with caution, for any student, but especially those learning a new language. These data points should be considered in conjunction with all other information collected about the student. |
| *Relying only on English language proficiency data to make decisions without gathering or analyzing information about a learner's proficiency in other languages.* | The first check-point for data should be to learn as much as you can about the student's achievement, culture, and learning behaviors in L1. Use multi-lingual assessments in L1 and English, or screeners that help illuminate language dominance, if possible. |
| *Having a closed mindset around "either/or." For example, the student must be identified as needing EAL support OR Learning Support.* | Put student needs, not school structures, at the center of a collaborative and multi-disciplinary approach. |
| *Allowing conditional enrollment based on* | Commit and collaborate; all children can learn. Enhancing a program in order to meet |

| *learning performance.* | students' needs improves the program for everyone. |
| --- | --- |
| *Using "morefferentiation" instead of differentiation for ELLs who struggle. Doing the same intervention over and over, or giving more of the same in-class instruction, when it is not producing results.* | Sometimes higher intensity or extra practice works well. Set a timeline to review progress in light of extra practice. Decide and hold yourselves accountable as a team as to when it will be time to do something different. |
| *Lowering expectations for students receiving EAL or Learning Support services.* | Teach all students to a high standard. Keep the bar where it belongs at a high level; scaffold, differentiate, and accommodate students utilizing their strengths. |
| *Denying all students in EAL and/or Learning Support the opportunity to study a World Language over the course of enrollment.* | Decisions about additional World Languages should be based on the picture of the whole child and his or her needs and situation. Schedules, logistics, and the demand on student time need to be considered when making programming decisions about all academic content for students, and no doors should be closed due to a particular label. |

Effective schools for culturally and linguistically diverse students must create a positive, inclusive school culture. Students' languages and cultures should be regarded as resources rather than problems or barriers (Sanchez-Lopez, 2012). All languages are valued, and multilingualism is regarded as an asset. Children who are fluent bilinguals outperform their monolingual peers on measures of metalinguistic and executive functioning skills (Paradis, Genesee, & Crago, 2011). Valuing home languages, and supporting parents in maintaining and developing home language proficiency for their children, clearly demonstrates the cognitive advantages of additive bilingualism.

**Knowing Ourselves**

One of the inconvenient truths of the classroom is that teachers need to know both their students and themselves. And it is often less challenging to know someone else than it is to come to know yourself. The great novelist, Joseph Conrad, wrote that the only thing more perilous than the journey into self is not undertaking it. In order to best serve our students, we need to be clear about our own identities, especially when we view ourselves as individual "specialist" teachers.

We also know that one of the non-negotiables of effective differentiation is coming to know our students as learners at a deep level. What we are now coming to understand is that the assumptions and mental models that we teachers bring to the table can skew our perceptions to the point where the "real" Mai, Ahmed, and Fang Wou are unrecognizable.

We all hold assumptions about learning, intelligence, student motivation and best practice in the classroom. Many of these assumptions are held at unconscious levels and have therefore escaped conscious examination, analysis and re-assessment. Even though these assumptions may be unexamined, they exert enormous influence over our behavior and decision-making. For example, the teacher who announces that, "Not everyone can get an A in my class" may have developed a mental model in which the assessment of student achievement is comparative and may be fostering a climate of unhealthy competition. Or the teacher who averages student grades over the semester in order to calculate a summative grade, may be unwittingly rewarding students who "get it first" and therefore be turning classroom learning into a mastery race.

In order to surface our assumptions about students, particularly those who are struggling in our classroom we need to engage in a rigorous examination of our practices, as well as the assumptions, values, and beliefs we hold. These constitute the fabric of our professional selves. Examining an assumption (e.g. "A student is either EAL or LS") and finding discomfort with that assumption, leads to a change in mindset. When we change our mindset, we transform ourselves. In truly outstanding schools, teachers and school leaders are constantly exploring who they are and designing whom they wish to become. We will explore the transformational nature of professional learning in greater depth in the section of this monograph Developing Professional Capacity.

### The Greatest Challenge

One of our greatest challenges in international schools is the effective inclusion of diverse learners. As our student populations become increasingly diverse, and as we become more knowledgeable about the needs of students and how to support them, it becomes more important to step back to look at the big picture. In order to significantly and positively impact the lives of children, we need to demonstrate the courage to follow our moral imperative by:

- Viewing students as individual children with varied and complex needs
- Identifying student strengths and building an asset-based approach
- Critically evaluating our systems and adjusting as needed

- Using culturally responsive and evidenced-based interventions
- Meeting the needs of the child and not the program

This "re-imagination" requires courage as well as intentional, explicit and rigorous teacher collaboration to meet student needs. This collaboration will not only help make the learning better for students, but provide opportunities for teacher and leader learning as well. It increases our capacity as educators and develops our organizational intelligence. Through team assessing, planning, and teaching we see multiple perspectives and hone our craft in profound ways. "EAL support has been increasingly viewed as an integrated process rather than a discrete discipline. When disciplinary boundaries overlap, it introduces powerful new ways of engaging with colleagues" (Nordmeyer, 2010).

Re-imagining will undoubtedly shift people's comfort zones, question teacher roles and identity, and possibly cause initial frustration as powerful change often does. We hope that this resource will help practitioners and leaders to define, design, deliver, and demonstrate optimal learning for students. We need to lean into this challenge, to discover who our learners are and what they need, so that we can provide the best and most appropriate services.

---

Key Ideas:
- We can expect that some students learning English will also demonstrate learning challenges.
- We need to re-imagine the question, "Should this student be served by EAL *or* LS?" to… "How can Learning Support *and* EAL work together to meet the needs of this student?"
- This re-imagination requires courage as well as intentional, explicit, and rigorous teacher collaboration to meet the needs of students.

## PART II: DESIGNING AND DELIVERING SUPPORTS

### Building Inclusive Schools

As international schools become increasingly inclusive, it is important to understand how ELLs fit into school-wide systems intended to serve students with learning differences. How can we meet the needs of culturally and linguistically diverse students within an inclusive school? Consider this classroom scenario:

> *Hyun Ki walks into his eighth grade Humanities class and is greeted by Ms. Wagner, his EAL teacher and Mr. Xu, his Humanities teacher who are setting up the class. While students complete the warm up connection to yesterday's lesson by writing an important fact on a sticky note and clustering them on the whiteboard, Hyun Ki laughs and talks with a classmate until he is prompted to work. They discuss an important fact in Korean and then compose a note in English to be added to the collection.*
>
> *Next, while Mr. Xu introduces a video clip to frame today's lesson, Ms. Wagner clusters the sticky notes and identifies any misconceptions. The students complete a pre-during-post observation task with a graphic organizer and conclude by discussing in small groups. Hyun Ki is the last student to transition to the new activity and Ms. Wagner helps him organize his materials and provides a sentence starter for the task.*
>
> *After the observation task, Ms. Wagner explains several key ideas that were misunderstood by students in the lesson warm up. Mr. Xu introduces a reading task and distributes three texts at different levels. Hyun Ki and three other classmates join a guided reading group facilitated by Ms. Wagner, which she will continue in EAL class later that day. Hyun Ki sits on one of the wobbly chairs in the classroom that supports his need for movement. When Ms. Wagner notices that Hyun Ki becomes distracted she moves in closer and touches his hand, providing a non-intrusive reminder to return to the task.*
>
> *As the class ends with five minutes to write an exit ticket, Ms. Wagner reminds Hyun Ki to make a note in the behavior log in the back of his homework notebook, reflecting on time-on-task, and providing data that his parents and the Student Support Team will discuss in next week's progress meeting.*

Hyun Ki is still acquiring academic English while learning grade-level content and he benefits from an intentional, collaborative, and integrated approach. It is clear that his native language is utilized as a tool for learning. Teachers work together to build formative assessment and differentiation into every lesson, which benefit all students; this also helps to engage Hyun Ki while allowing teachers to monitor his progress. His language development is supported by specific teaching strategies integrated into his content classes and the EAL teacher assesses his academic language development regularly. For the past three months, a solution-focused team including the EAL teacher, Learning Support teacher, Hyun Ki and his parents have met to build on his strengths and provide guidance to support his learning.

As independent, international schools, we have the opportunity to define our own programs and establish our own best practices. This is a daunting responsibility, but this same autonomy can also allow schools to provide courageous leadership in building inclusive programs to serve all students, including ELLs.

**Accessibility and Differentiation** (Why not start with identification and intervention?)

While a school's journey of support for an individual student often begins with assessment or recommendations for strategic interventions, the authors of this monograph made a conscious decision to begin our discussion with a systemic view and whole-school approach. Indeed when any student steps into our school, he or she encounters the whole school, and by definition, inclusive schools must consider how they build the general program to serve *all* students.

Accessibility is the foundation of an effective program to serve culturally and linguistically diverse students; high quality, evidence-based instruction should be available to every student in every classroom. The principle of Universal Design, which has come to education via architecture, holds that an accommodation which is intended for a specific population often has a much wider benefit when it is universally designed to serve the entire population. For example, curb ramps originally intended for wheelchairs benefit everyone, including skateboards, bicycles, and strollers. Likewise, before we can consider specialized programs or interventions for any one student, we must ensure that all students have access to the best teaching and learning we can offer.

As international schools become more inclusive, with increasing numbers of ELLs and students with learning disabilities, differentiation plays a key role in understanding and meeting the needs of diverse learners. Differentiation values the complex learning profiles of all students and incorporates those profiles into instructional planning and assessment practices. Differentiation provides multiple entry points to learning where most student needs will be met through effective core instruction. When ELLs struggle, we must first inquire whether the instructional environment is sufficiently differentiated and accessible before trying to determine if the student has a learning difference.

Assessment, core curriculum, instruction, and collaboration are embedded elements of differentiation. Knowing students as learners means knowing how they learn best; understanding areas of strength and challenge, interests, cultural values, gender implications, and language history. Clearly defined learning standards provide teachers the in-depth knowledge of concepts needed to differentiate instruction - to understand what is essential learning for all students. "A broad, research-based repertoire of instructional strategies is a vital component in the differentiated classroom. Effective instructional strategies triangulate the three critical features of the classroom: the learning outcomes, the curriculum content, and the students themselves" (Powell & Kusuma-Powell, 2007).

Differentiation is a complex and highly demanding process that requires collaboration in order to design accessible and meaningful learning for all students. In short, differentiation produces diverse learners with access to the curriculum and an invitation to learn. Differentiation, however, is not possible without effective assessment practices:

- *Formative assessment* is a process, rather than a tool, which provides in-the-moment learning information about a student's growth, strengths and weaknesses; formative assessment helps teachers to adjust instruction and make important decisions about how best to differentiate learning. For ELLs, regular verbal and nonverbal comprehension checks are essential. These "hinge questions" (Wiliam, 2015) are a key part of contingent pedagogy (DeBarger et al, 2011), allowing teachers to determine when to move on, when to review, and for whom.

- *Interim assessments* provide checkpoints of student learning growth at key points during the year. For ELLs, these should provide information about student growth against established benchmarks or expectations in both language acquisition and core curricular areas. Monitoring student progress towards these benchmarks ensures that students who are not following typical pathways of English acquisition are identified so that support can be provided in a timely and responsive way.

- *Summative assessments* used to measure progress at the end of a period of learning must also be differentiated. ELLs may need accommodations (e.g. extra time, use of a dictionary or electronic translator), which should be similar to the strategies used throughout the unit of learning. Other strategies might include providing students multiple ways to demonstrate knowledge, skill, and understanding with choices of task where appropriate. This does not mean ELLs are let "off the language hook" or that the standard is lowered in terms of conceptual understanding, but that we differentiate assessment in a way that gives the best picture of their understanding *while* simultaneously pushing them to improve expressive language.

The regular use of collaborative data practices such as those described in *Processes and Tools to Support Data-Driven Decision Making in Learning Support* (2015) can be useful not only at the student level, but also at the program level. Regularly analyzing the progress of ELLs on interim and summative and/or external measures will help school teams develop a sense of what typical pathways look like for their ELL students.

Student progress data should also be used to evaluate the effectiveness of the program as a whole and plan for improvements. In Multi-tiered Models of Support such as Response to Intervention (explained in detail below), a high quality core program will be effective for approximately 80% of students. Therefore, if more than 20% of ELLs are not making typical progress, the match between the components of the core program and the ELL population characteristics should be reviewed.

**Collaboration to Support Student Learning**

A diverse population of students with a range of learning needs requires dedicated, compassionate professional adults who work together to serve student learning. In inclusive international schools, structural and cultural support for professional collaboration is necessary to engage all learners in the core curriculum. Roland Barth asserts, "One incontrovertible finding emerges from my career spent working in and around schools: The nature of relationships among the adults within a school has a greater influence on the character and quality of that school and on student accomplishment than anything else" (2006). Collaboration is not an end in itself, but collaboration can improve student learning and transform schools.

Since ELLs need to develop content and language skills at the same time, changing models of EAL support have required professional cooperation between specialists and mainstream teachers. Greater integration and collaboration has challenged all teachers to view ELLs along a developmental continuum of academic English, and has reframed the role of EAL teachers. Viewing ELLs as a small, separate group of students who are the sole responsibility of EAL teachers is neither effective nor just. In the past, ELLs were considered a "problem" for the EAL teacher to "fix" so they could return to the mainstream to learn the "regular" curriculum with other students. Current better practice dictates that *all* teachers share responsibility for *all* students. When all teachers recognize a collective responsibility to serve all English language learners, including those with learning differences, collaboration is not a luxury but a necessity.

As EAL teachers within inclusive international schools become more collaborative, they serve as team members, professional resources and sometimes coaches for colleagues. EAL, Learning Support, and core teachers are equal and essential parts of the team of teachers responsible for all students. Using specific tools for collaboration allows teachers to work in concert to support student learning and professional growth:

- *Working agreements* can help to build relational trust and define roles and responsibilities for the purpose of greater student learning.
- A "menu" of support options can define what is possible and provides a convenient tool for co-planning, co-teaching, and co-assessing.
- Electronic tools such as shared calendars, Google docs, and collaborative curriculum maps can support asynchronous co-planning and co-assessing to complement face-to-face meetings.

These tools can help establish a trusting relationship by facilitating the intentional examination of how teachers work together, and periodically revisiting them helps to maintain mutual respect.

Finally, international schools are unique in that they include programs across divisions, often on the same campus. A lack of collaboration may result in disjointed programs or inconsistent school cultures. "Students and their families may feel like they encounter an international border crossing when they transition from fifth to sixth grade or from middle school to high school; it is as if they need to translate signs, exchange currency or obtain a visa for admission to the next division" (Nordmeyer 2015). On the other hand, collaboration between divisions to support alignment builds consistent programs and shared community practices and values. By extending common policies and practices across all divisions, transitions become less stressful and families benefit from continuity of services.

## Using a Multi-tiered System of Support to Identify Learning Needs of ELLs

For more than a decade now, special education leadership has offered an alternative to the psychometric/medical model for identification of learning disabilities. This intervention driven approach is typically referred to as a Multi-tiered System of Support (MTSS) or Response to

Intervention approach (RTI). There are several compelling reasons to consider this approach when determining whether or not an ELL student requires Learning Support services.

The traditional psychometric approach to identifying and referring students to special education has significant restrictions. Most models depend on tests that have limited evidence for use with students who are culturally or linguistically different from the normative group for which the assessment was designed. Learning disabilities research over the last three decades is relatively inconclusive, and most studies have examined correlates, rather than causes. At this point, it is hard to suggest anything beyond academic underachievement as the primary defining characteristic of a learning disability (Vanderwood M. L. NASP 2014).

To fully understand RTI/MTSS, the reader needs to be familiar with the following terms:

- A universal screener refers to a brief assessment tool that is intended to efficiently identify students who are developing specific skills. The test is administered to all students in a grade level. One or more cut-off scores are determined and students falling below a cut-off and possibly above a second cut off are identified to receive a specific level of intervention. In some cases the universal screener is used in conjunction with other data to determine the level of intervention needed. The same assessment is typically used for progress monitoring.
- Progress monitoring refers to the process of systematically re-assessing a student to determine growth. More sophisticated measures will measure expected growth.
- Tier 1 refers to the core instruction that all students receive.
- Tier 2 refers to short-term, targeted interventions that are used to address the needs of students who show evidence of needing intervention that is beyond the core instruction. That is, students who do not make progress with Tier 1 alone receive Tier 2 interventions in addition to Tier 1.
- Tier 3 refers to a level of intervention that is more intensive, individualized, or longer term than the preceding tiers. Tier 3 interventions are intended for students who do not respond to Tier 2 interventions. In many schools this is the equivalent of special education and typically involves an individualized education plan.

When implementing RTI/MTSS in a school with a culturally and linguistically diverse population, the WIDA Consortium (2013) explains that:

- The core instruction in Tier 1 for ELLs should be delivered in classrooms with teachers who are knowledgeable about the process of acquiring a second or additional language (Hill & Flynn, 2006), and know how to deliver culturally relevant content, literacy, and language instruction.

- *Instruction within these settings would not be viewed as an intervention (Tiers 2 or 3), but rather part of ELLs' core instruction (National Center on Response to Intervention, 2011).*

Current research concerning the efficacy of applying an MTSS process to identify ELL students who require additional support in developing literacy skills has drawn several conclusions. The points made and the research referred to in this section concern literacy skills with early elementary age students (K-3). The studies referred to involved Spanish speaking ELL students in the United States. These studies need to be duplicated with other linguistic groups in other settings. However, without evidence to the contrary, the findings do support our consideration when deciding how to assure success with English literacy for our ELL students:

- Present universal screening tools are effective in identifying literacy delays in ELLs. These same universal screeners are also effective for use as a measure of progress monitoring. These tests are as good at identifying literacy delays and progress in ELLs as they are with native English speakers (Healy, Vanderwood, & Edelston 2005).
- In the early grades, ELL students can develop English literacy skills simultaneously as they develop English language skills. In other words, development of basic reading skills for ELL students is not predicted by English language proficiency  (Lesaux and Siegal 2003).
- Literacy remediation must not replace English language instruction or core instruction; it is never in place of core instruction for ELL instruction (Vaughn et al 2006).
- Literacy reinforcement with ELLs must include vocabulary building (Gersten & Geva, 2003).
- Phonological awareness instruction has the most significant impact on literacy skill development with both ELL and native English speakers (Chiappe, Siegel, & Wade-Woolley 2002).

Learning Support teachers should not be supplementing a lack of high quality core instruction, and as stated above, EAL teachers should not be cutting into their English language instruction to teach core literacy skills. Classroom teachers are often stretched to "fit in" all that is expected, but literacy instruction for all students should not be sacrificed. One way to assess the quality of Tier 1 instruction from the perspective of an ELL student is to shadow an ELL student for a day to determine how much direct literacy instruction the student receives throughout the day and compare that with the typical non-ELL student. If it is found that literacy instruction is less than it is for non-ELL students, an instructional dilemma is present.

Because an MTSS approach is more focused on intervention than obtaining a diagnosis, there may be a number of ELL students who receive early intervention services for literacy who do not qualify as having a significant learning disability. Therefore, data needs to be looked at continuously. Progress monitoring is essential; ELLs' progress can vary considerably. Many students will make rapid progress and will no longer require additional reinforcement (Vanderwood M. L. NASP 2015).

**Core Program for ELLs**

An asset-based comprehensive system of support for ELLs should be based on the premise that all students can learn, that we should build on student strengths and that all students should have access to best-practice and differentiated core instruction within the general education classroom. "Teaching and learning should revolve around who our language learners are, what they can do and how we can benefit from the tremendous assets they bring to school" (Gottlieb 2013). In addition to high-quality, culturally responsive, differentiated instruction in all classrooms, ELLs may receive academic language support services such as Bilingual Education, Dual Language Instruction, Sheltered Instruction, or EAL pull-out/push-in support. The goal of this support is to assist students in simultaneously learning English while learning *in* English.

International schools should have an explicit language policy which values and promotes multilingualism as a social, cultural, and academic asset. Schools should educate parents about the value of bilingualism and how to support language development at home. For ELLs who struggle academically, the home language is an essential tool. It provides insight into a student's learning, helps students access grade-level content, and promotes the development of academic English. All teachers should be educated about the appropriate use of students' home languages in an international school classroom. Finally, a student's home language is intimately connected to his or her identity; no one should be asked to check his home language at the door when they enter an inclusive international school. All languages should be valued in an international school community and ELLs should be encouraged to develop their home language.

In schools with a large majority of a single home language, or where all students speak the same home language, there may be considerations of classroom management. When research meets reality, educators may wonder whether encouraging home language actually detracts from the use of English. It is important in this case for teachers to engage students through performance assessments in English. For example, if a small group of native Turkish speakers working together recognize that they will each need to use English to defend their opinion to the class, they will be more likely to use English to rehearse their answers. Teachers can also develop students' metacognition by asking about language choices. If a pair of students is using a common home language to complete a task, the teacher might inquire whether the students are clarifying concepts, discussing the task, or just being social. Both teachers and students need to be aware of the reasons behind language choices.

## Addressing Structural Constraints

Many international schools have unintentionally created structural or programmatic constraints that may impede the effectiveness of providing services for ELLs who struggle academically. The consequences of our decisions often create inflexible systems that force us into the false dichotomy of assigning students to either EAL or Learning Support. Schools must consider external and self-imposed barriers in order to design intentional programs to facilitate an asset-based and collaborative approach to serving ELLs with a range of learning needs.

*Additional fees:* Some international schools charge additional fees for students that receive EAL instruction and Learning Support. Fee structures often require that a student be served by one program or the other. A one-time fee has less impact on program design than a fee-for-service approach which can place enormous pressure on students, teachers, and parents and often limits flexible and responsive program design.

*School schedules:* School and division schedules can make scheduling ELLs in appropriate classes challenging, possibly leading to limited course options and restricted access to core curriculum. By scheduling students who receive EAL or Learning Support first, counselors are able to ensure students are placed in the appropriate classes with qualified teachers who have the skills and experience to meet their needs.

*Contact architecture:* The location of EAL and Learning Support in proximity to one another influences the degree in which collaboration occurs. The contact architecture of a school can facilitate or inhibit the degree of collaboration that occurs. The location of professionals within a building impacts patterns of interaction. When teachers work near each other, they see one another more often, observe each other's practice, and spontaneous hallway conversations happen more readily.

When Shanghai American School relocated its high school EAL program from the third floor at the far end of the high school to the first floor of the school, near the main entrance and across from the Learning Support room, collaboration was a natural result. ELLs who received Learning Support moved back and forth between both classrooms, and teachers shared both intervention strategies and student learning data. Because the EAL classroom also served as the Writing Center for all students in the high school, it became a hub for collaborative literacy development. Students from the full range of English proficiency stopped in for feedback or for an impromptu peer tutoring session. When mainstream teachers needed to visit EAL or Learning Support, they had the chance to check in with both teachers conveniently.

The International School Bangkok experienced a similar increase in collaboration as a result of physical proximity when the EAL and Learning Support departments were relocated to the Student Services Hub, located on the ground floor next to the math quad. The open plan space is surrounded by breakout rooms and classrooms, with areas designated for silent, individual work, and collaborative group work. Students who do not receive services from the EAL and Learning Support departments also choose to work and seek support from teachers in this inviting learning space, which provides opportunities for new social interactions and connections.

**Staffing and resources**: A lack of resources - both material and human - may impede effective program design and delivery. EAL and Learning Support teachers may compete for limited resources. One program may refuse to take on more students than the other program; or one program attempts to build their numbers in order to maintain or add staffing. Although many international schools require flexible and creative deployment of their teachers due to limited staffing, assigning untrained teachers to EAL or Learning Support classes without adequate professional knowledge is not only ineffective but unethical.

**Exclusionary or vague policies**: International schools often lack cohesive and documented policies to guide program implementation. The result leads to ambiguous practices such as the misidentification of student learning profiles and arbitrary placement in either an EAL *or* Learning Support program, rather than EAL *and* Learning Support, when necessary.

## Design Considerations

Department structures can enhance collaboration and/or implementation of effective instruction for struggling ELLs. Learning Support and EAL teachers have historically been marginalized faculty members, working in isolation and with little coordination and collaboration within their own departments or with other departments in the school. One important question involves how to organize EAL and Learning Support specialists. Where will the department live? Who will supervise them? Where will they be located and where will they serve students?

In some international schools, EAL and Learning Support are part of a larger Student Support Team or unified department. Some schools with increasingly diverse student populations target dual-certified teachers who can support a variety of needs in the classroom. In either case, consistent structures and protocols for collaborative planning can support teachers and help to reduce barriers and build a common process for identification, documentation, and communication of student needs and support programs. "Parties who see different aspects of a problem can constructively explore their differences and search for solutions that go beyond their own limited vision of what is possible" Gray (1989). Together, EAL and Learning Support teachers can promote effective scaffolding for diverse learners and improve differentiation for all students.

In each of the models below, increased collaboration between EAL and Learning Support specialists brings a clearer perspective to both inquiry and advocacy. When students are viewed through both lenses, everyone benefits from a better understanding of a student's strengths and needs.

| Program Design | Collaborative Contributions | Collaborative Considerations |
|---|---|---|
| *"cousins"*<br>*separate departments*<br><br>EAL  Learning Support | Positive professional relationships between individuals across departments can help facilitate collaboration. This often happens organically and can be built by intentionally designating meeting structures with cross-department representation. | If left to develop organically, these relationships take time. Bringing the two departments together periodically to understand each other's work and build professional relationships helps to develop trust and common approaches to serving students. |
| *"siblings"*<br>*two separate departments as part of a larger Student Services department*<br>**Student Services**<br>EAL  Learning Support | A single umbrella department of Student Services can help to coordinate systems and collaborative structures such as Student Support Teams and processes for organizing student data. If there is a single Student Services Director, a voice on the school leadership team can provide both inquiry and advocacy. | When Learning Support and EAL teachers stand together under the same umbrella, collaborative relationships form more naturally. A greater understanding of one another's expertise is a positive consequence of belonging to the same larger department. Further, the Student Services Director can facilitate the development of shared procedures and policies. |
| *"overlapping"*<br>*two separate departments with some teachers belonging to both* | When some teachers are dual-certified, and bring expertise from both EAL and Learning Support, they can help to build collaboration by serving as a bridge to both departments. These individuals can help to interpret student learning | These specialists with dual certification often share similar philosophies and understandings about student learning. This synchronous perspective leads to natural collaboration. It helps systems move away from |

| | | |
|---|---|---|
| EAL / Learning Support (Venn diagram with ★) | data from both perspectives. | either/or placements and rather focuses efforts on the needs of students. |
| *"hybrid" or "dual service"* one unified department (EAL & Learning Support circle) | Teachers who are dual-certified or have both EAL and Learning Support backgrounds can serve ELLs with disabilities. These individuals can help to interpret student learning data from both perspectives. (Note: this does not imply an overall reduction in staffing.) | Students who need only EAL support or Learning Support may not have their needs served in this model if it limits the total number of teachers available for a specific group of students or at a specific time of the day. However, the degree of collaboration is still high owing to similar philosophies and approaches to learning. |

ELLs with learning disabilities deserve qualified teachers who are able to address their cultural, linguistic, and learning needs. These teachers should use teaching methods and materials that are known to be effective both with students with disabilities and ELLs (Cloud, 2006). Placing these students in EAL support that does not meet their learning needs, or Learning Support that does not address their language needs, is neither effective nor principled.

**Build on Strengths and Assets:** Evidence-based assessment and instruction of language learners with disabilities should identify and build on student strengths. The WIDA Consortium's (2013) "Can Do Philosophy" is a specific articulation of how an asset-based approach helps students, teachers, parents, and school leaders design programs and individual instructional plans based on what culturally and linguistically diverse students bring to the educational context. With this "glass half full" mindset, educators can identify and build on a student's strengths to help the learner to develop in other areas. On the other hand, decisions about student support are often dictated by the deficit model, or the assumption that there is something "wrong" with students who don't learn at an expected rate. Educators in international schools must challenge this assumption and tap into the strength areas of their ELLs. Understanding a student's areas of strength and passion is critical in determining the most effective interventions and service delivery options.

---

**Samantha's strengths**

*Samantha struggles with reading fluency and decoding in English. Reading out loud in front of the class reduces her to tears and she requires extended time to complete much of her work because of the length of time it takes to read the material. However, Samantha excels in theater and has shown an affinity for the dramatic. Although it takes her time to read through and memorize a script, often requiring someone to read it aloud to her and discuss concepts and vocabulary in her home language, Samantha has shown a strong ability to remember her lines and deliver them with emotion and timing. Tapping into Samantha's strength and passion for drama is a way to value her interests and abilities. Allowing Samantha to demonstrate her learning in alternate ways related to performance and drama would provide teachers a more accurate assessment of her depth of understanding and allow Samantha to maintain her status among her peers.*

---

Recognizing student strengths and helping them see their capabilities facilitates a positive learning experience, thus motivating students to persevere through their challenge areas and appreciate and acknowledge their strengths as learners.

*Parent Engagement:* For culturally and linguistically diverse students who struggle academically, it is critical to involve parents in school. Parents are their child's first teacher and know their strengths and challenges; they can provide information about a student's background and learning history. The home school partnership is critical in supporting parents whose home cultures may have different attitudes or approaches to learning needs and related support than those held by the school. Parents should be guided to "consistently use their most proficient language with their child using communication that is developmentally appropriate for their child" (Cloud, 2006).

Key Ideas:

- As international schools become increasingly inclusive, it is important to understand how ELLs and students with learning disabilities fit into schoolwide systems of support. We have the opportunity and responsibility to define and design programs that are collaborative and adaptive.
- A comprehensive system of support for ELLs and students with learning disabilities should be based on the premise that all students can learn and should have access to differentiated core instruction within the general education classroom.
- Using a Multi-tiered System of Support offers students staged, collaboratively developed interventions, with close progress monitoring. Tiered responses allow schools to be adaptive as they learn about their students, and when managed with fidelity, can reduce the number of students mis-identified with learning disabilities.
- ELLs with learning disabilities deserve qualified, specialized teachers who are able to address their cultural, linguistic, and learning needs.
- When we recognize our collective responsibility to serve all English language learners, including those with learning differences, collaboration is not a luxury but a necessity (Nordmeyer 2015).

## PART III: IDENTIFICATION AND INTERVENTIONS

### Identification of ELLs and Learning Needs

English Language Learners are a multilingual population of students with a myriad of cultural and experiential backgrounds. As international school educators, it is imperative to identify what typical and nontypical learning pathways look like for these students. We must further explore the appropriate "look fors" when expected progress is not made in the varying contexts of our learners and consider factors that impact language acquisition for each individual's language learning context.

*Casey is a second grade student who is mid-way through the school year at International School of the World. He is originally from Thailand and has attended ISW since he was three years of age. His parents report that Casey's Thai language development is typical and they are keen for him to become proficient in English. They appreciate the confidence Casey has gained in English communication.*

*At school, Casey receives high-quality classroom instruction and his language development is supported through meaningful collaboration between his EAL, classroom, and specialist teachers. The team strives to incorporate Casey's home language and culture as often as possible in their instruction. The teachers note that Casey is well liked by his peers and appreciate his positive attitude towards school.*

*Casey's teachers agree that his oral language proficiency seems to be at the typical rate of development for an ELL student. They have observed that he uses both social and academic vocabulary with confidence. His sentence structures are becoming more complex and he shows few hesitations as he speaks. While obvious oral language progress is noted, teachers express concern that Casey's written language development is lagging relative to other ELLs of a similar background. During reading instruction, Casey is easily distracted and appears to be unmotivated. Concepts of print are established, but Casey does not yet remember all single letter sounds. This is evident when he attempts to decode words in reading and when he sounds out words during the writing process. Casey has not yet developed sufficient phonetic skills and relies on whole word reading. Teachers are voicing concerns with the discrepancy between oral*

> *and written language progress and are considering if Casey would benefit from additional literacy intervention.*
>
> *To further explore this discrepancy, the classroom teacher's next step is to share Casey's areas of strength and areas of developmental concern with a multi-perspective team (for example, a Student Support Team).*

## Factors that Impact Language Acquisition

ELLs progress through the same stages of language acquisition, but do so at varying rates. Typically language acquisition is broken down into four stages that range from an initial silent period through to proficiency, where language learners are able to converse proficiently, have increased comprehension, and a more expansive vocabulary. At times, students may make insufficient progress with their language acquisition despite quality classroom instruction characterized by the following:

- cultural awareness
- integration of home language
- collaborative practices between classroom and EAL teachers
- differentiated instruction and flexible grouping
- on-going progress monitoring.

When we recognize that the instruction integrates these characteristics, it is necessary to also examine the individual student's strengths and how we are building upon these areas of strength in our current instructional practices. More specifically, teachers and schools may need to reconsider how a student's assets can be utilized in meeting his or her needs and the effectiveness of interventions implemented. For example, if a reading intervention does not incorporate a student's high verbal skills or passion for bird-watching, it is a lost opportunity.

As reflective practitioners, it is also important to be cognizant of the distinctions between typical and nontypical progress of ELLs with similar backgrounds. Sometimes it is easy to assume that a student is acquiring language at a slower rate and to simply accept this; however, it is also necessary to take into consideration that perhaps the student's slower rate may reflect a learning difference. For this reason, it is essential to gather as much information as possible about a student in the home language, including any psychoeducational testing, as well as a student's language proficiency in reading, writing, speaking and listening; if a native speaker of the home language is available for an informal language assessment, this information can complement a home language survey. A complete picture of a student's assets and needs cannot be built without this essential information.

Paradis, Genesee & Crago (2004) assert that dual language learners differ from each other in two important respects:

1. Whether they are members of a majority or minority ethnolinguistic community.
2. Whether they learned two or more languages simultaneously from infancy (simultaneous bilingualism) or learn the second once the first is established (sequential bilingualism).

|  | **Majority group** | **Minority group** |
|---|---|---|
| **Simultaneous bilinguals** | Both languages widely spoken/high status | One or both languages not widely spoken/not high status |
| **Sequential bilinguals** | First language is widely spoken/high status<br><br>Education through the second language/may be majority or minority language of the community | First language is not widely spoken/high status<br><br>Education through the second language/majority language of the community or wider region |

*Types of dual language learners from Paradis, Genesee & Crago (2004)*

The majority or minority status of the child's first and second language may influence language outcomes because the size and status of the speech community impacts opportunities for input in a particular language.

The age at which the second language is introduced is important because research shows different outcomes depending on when a new language is introduced. While both the quantity and quality of language exposure are important factors, students who start learning a second language at a younger age have more success. Simultaneous bilinguals usually acquire both languages in the home, whereas sequential bilinguals usually have different home and community languages, which also has implications for language acquisition.

Given these parameters, "typical" pathways of English language acquisition emerge for the majority of ELLs. Students whose growth deviates from these expected pathways might raise red flags. Factors to consider include:

- rate of learning compared to students of a comparable background.
- unbalanced language proficiency: outliers in one or more skill areas.
- quality of English enrichment (educational history or current home/school environment).
- early history of speech and language problems.
- difficulties/delays in both L1 & L2.
- circumstances related to the transition to a new school and culture.

## Classroom Challenges for ELLs

ELLs may struggle in a classroom when English is the medium of instruction: learning English while learning *in English* is double the work (Short & Fitzsimmons, 2007). It is helpful, therefore, to be able to recognize typical learning pathways for ELLs in international schools. ELLs run the risk of being both over-identified and under-identified as having learning needs. In schools with a lower proportion of ELLs, there is a tendency to over-identify ELLs as having learning needs.

ELLs typically take five to seven years or longer to acquire the academic English skills needed to thrive in the regular classroom (Goldenberg, 2013). This presents a dilemma: On the one hand, not allowing sufficient time for students to acquire important skills before referring them for evaluation for Learning Support eligibility can result in them being incorrectly identified as having learning needs. On the other hand, waiting too long to act when a student is not following a typical pathway can result in ELLs being under-identified. This tends to happen more frequently in schools with higher numbers of ELLs. This is sometimes seen in the "paradox of fifth grade" when elementary teachers who suspect that "something else is going on" want to investigate before the student moves to middle school. Often educators wait until the student has developed enough English skills to determine whether the learning pathway is typical, yet at this late stage, precious time for implementation of specific interventions has been lost.

The sociocultural context is a critical factor in language acquisition and each learner follows a unique developmental pathway. While it is essential to understand second language acquisition as a product of a student's home language, culture, and environment, educators in international schools often see common patterns in how students from similar backgrounds develop academic English. With this in mind, knowing some of the characteristics that differentiate between language acquisition behaviors and learning disabilities can be useful in identifying a student's strengths and individual needs.

When a student struggles, our first question should be "Is there a mismatch between the school's approach and the student's needs?" Second language acquisition can be delayed due to a number of factors. Factors to consider include: culture, personality, age, environment, relationships, family dynamics, quality/quantity of L1 schooling, possible learning disabilities, and transition to a new school and country.

When a delay in language acquisition is observed, it might be attributed to a learning difference (Christo, Borisov, Sibert 2013). ELLs may exhibit learning behaviors that appear similar to those behaviors observed in students with learning difficulties. Some well established markers for distinguishing typical development versus a possible learning difference can serve as a useful resource for teachers.

### Similarities Between Language Acquisition and Learning Disabilities

| *What you might see in the classroom* | *Explanation based on second language acquisition development* | *Indicator of a possible learning disability* |
|---|---|---|
| Difficulty understanding academic English | Makes steady progress in developing academic English | Progress is uneven or inconsistent |
| Difficulty expressing ideas when writing in English | Writing skills in English develop over time with oral language ability in English | Writing in English is very challenging and does not reflect oral ability in English |
| Difficulty expressing ideas when speaking in English | Able to communicate in L1 more easily than in English | Difficulty communicating in both L1 and English due to an expressive language disorder |
| Does not follow a series of directions in English | Directions are not well understood | Poor short-term memory or lack of attention |
| Difficulty distinguishing between sounds in English | English sounds not in student's L1 | Lacks phonological awareness even though the student knows the sounds |
| Difficulty decoding words in | Sound-symbol | May seem to know letter |

| English | correspondence in English different than in L1 | sounds one day and not the next |
| --- | --- | --- |
| Delay in response to questions in English | Student may be translating question in mind before responding in L2; gradual improvement seen over time | Student consistently takes a longer time period to respond in L1 & L2; may be due to a processing speed deficit |

**Adapted from Klingner and Eppolito, 2014; Adelson, Geva, and Fraser, 2014**

Once it is determined that a student is having challenges that are unexpected despite access to high quality instruction we move to the next phase of the process. As established in the introduction of this document, our students do not fit neatly into categories, but for organizational purposes we place them into designated programs. Nevertheless, by maintaining the position that every student is unique and brings his or her own experiences into play, we are freed up to consider what each student needs, regardless of program designation. To accomplish this, a systematic investigation is needed in order to determine whether additional support, interventions, or accommodations are required.

To ensure that student needs are identified it is important to gather descriptive data across multiple areas. Comprehensive data collection will more likely build a holistic profile of the learner which can lead to optimal instruction and intervention.

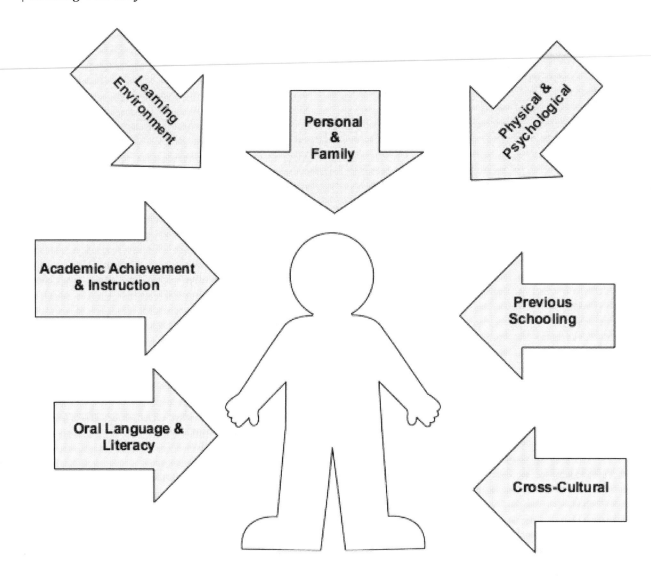

Comprehensive data collection crosses a range of areas and should be descriptive in form. It would benefit schools to develop protocols for gathering and considering these descriptive data points to better understand how these factors may impact student academic achievement, development of academic language, and interventions. As expanded upon by the WIDA Consortium (2014), the seven factors to consider when collecting data are:

1. ***Learning Environment:*** When examining factors that influence an ELL student's performance, international schools should consider individual and collective teacher expertise with regard to language acquisition. Appropriate and specific professional development and training to bolster teacher understanding of English language learning is necessary to ensure that teachers are equipped to meet the needs of a diverse population. Adequate instructional resources and spaces establish the optimal environment for students to access curriculum. Differentiated instruction in the

classroom is important in that it allows students multiple access points to the content and options for showing their learning. Additionally, schools can draw on student's home language and culture to help inform interventions.

2. ***Academic Achievement & Instruction:*** Having systematic integration of academic language and literacy within content areas must also be considered. Schools should be able to assess what students know and what they can do within content areas that is separate knowledge from language proficiency.

3. ***Oral Language & Literacy Practice:*** Schools benefit by gathering developmental histories of ELLs primary language acquisition, literacy in English and in the home language, and literacy for academic and social purposes. In gathering this information, schools can better determine if the student made typical progress prior to entering the current school environment.

4. ***Personal & Family:*** In addition to educational data points, it is imperative that schools gather information about the student's home life and prior experiences. Schools should explore a student's family dynamics, parental involvement, family and cultural expectations and aspirations, student interests, and experiential background.

5. ***Physical & Psychological:*** According to the WIDA Consortium, "Students' physical and psychological well-being is foundational and inextricably connected to their learning and how they feel at school" (18). With that in mind, schools should take into consideration extrinsic factors that influence students such as medical conditions, mental health, nutrition, social-emotional development, and sense of belonging. A culture that illustrates a growth mindset, the development of strong relationships, the embracing of diversity, and building of resilience are all fundamental to the development of the learning environment.

6. ***Previous Schooling:*** Gaining a clear understanding of the educational history of ELLs is vital in the data collection process as it can help schools determine if the student has had a cohesive educational experience. In gathering this information about past instructional programs, schools can identify whether the student has gaps in his or her educational history. This may be difficult as parents may fear the admissions process and withhold important information.

7. ***Cross-Cultural:*** Information about the acculturation of home-school and school-school expectations is important information to gather. Schools should place high value on

students' cultural identity and its impact on learning. Some schools build exploration of Third Culture Kids into the curriculum.

Information concerning the components stated above can be gathered through interviews with the student, teacher, and parents. The student file often contains helpful information and clues about the student's learning.

In addition, teams should gather observational data - from teachers or through direct observation - about the *student as a learner:*

- What is the child paying attention to and NOT paying attention to?
- What's the attention span in comparison to peers?
- What do we notice about the child's interactions/transactions within the classroom?
- What do we observe as the child's strengths in learning?

Considering a student's current learning behaviors in relation to the seven factors listed above will help to create a clearer picture of the student's learning pathway, what strengths he/she brings to the classroom, and previous strategies that have been beneficial.

Standardized assessments that are administered to all students and assessments that are administered only to students within specific programs should be reviewed and interpreted with caution. Even though these assessments typically are normed on a population that is different from the student's, useful descriptive information can still be obtained. However, when these standardized assessments are used to assess students who are not represented in the norming sample it is important to acknowledge the limitations and focus on the qualitative information they provide.

In some instances, an assessment can be administered in the student's primary language along with English. It is also very useful to have some level of informal assessment of the student's specific skill level in the primary language. This is particularly helpful when a school collects assessment and trajectory data on all students' progress in the EAL program. This is not only useful in assessing the program, it also allows us to gain a better sense of the typical pathway of language learning.

**Recommended Assessment Practices**

Conduct an assessment of the student's proficiency in their home language(s) and in English to determine their language proficiency in both and make recommendations about which language to administer formal psychoeducational assessments, if necessary. The assessment can be done using performance based measures such as story retelling, writing samples, observations, file reviews, and interviews with family and school personnel. This assessment should assess language acquisition and proficiency as well as higher level thinking skills. It may include an assessment of:

- receptive and expressive vocabulary
- oral communication ability
- reading comprehension
- story retelling ability
- writing skills

Examine the extrinsic factors that may be impacting language acquisition before concluding that the difficulties are due to an intrinsic language impairment (Gaviria & Tipton 2012). Whenever feasible, conduct an evaluation in the language most likely to yield accurate information about what the student knows and can do. In some cases this might be entirely in the ELL's home language (ideally by a bilingual assessor or with the help of a trained interpreter), in some cases in both the home language and in English, and in some cases in English only.

Select and administer assessment tools that are non-discriminatory and help to determine the extent to which a student has a learning disability, rather than assessing their English language skills. Use standardized, norm-referenced assessments with extreme caution, documenting any deviations from the standardized administration. In some cases only a qualitative interpretation will be appropriate. Use dynamic assessment techniques such as testing the limits, graduated prompting, and test-teach-retest.

Use a body of evidence to diagnose a disability and/or determine eligibility for Learning Support. This might include:

- performance-based assessment in the classroom
- observations by appropriate specialists (psychologists, speech language pathologists, special educators, etc.)
- information gathered from parents and other educators
- carefully interpreted assessment results

*The San Diego Unified School District CEP-EL Process Manual (2012) contains helpful sample student and parent interviews and observation protocols.

Once sufficient data has been collected we begin processing the information. We do this by making connections, discovering consistencies, and ruling out explanations; essentially, we are building a hypothesis. Once again, it is important to be aware of our own bias and assumptions. Our tendency is to see what we know to the exclusion of other explanations. To counter this tendency it is necessary to engage with a multi-disciplinary team throughout the process as much as possible. It is understood that full team participation is not always possible at each stage. However, there needs to be opportunity for team input before conclusions are drawn and an action plan is developed.

The Student Support Team should include the school professionals who work with the student or have been involved with gathering data or managing the referral. For efficiency, it is often useful to have information available in advance, but no decisions have been made prior to the meeting. It is important to reiterate that an effective team is student centered and solution focused.

The eventual outcome of an assessment is the development of a learner profile and an action plan. This would include an explanation of strengths and areas that need to be addressed through intervention. The development of a plan should begin by asking the question, *"What does the student need to be successful?"* The action plan for students who are English language learners and simultaneously experiencing other learning challenges often requires creativity and the willingness to cross over support systems; the consequence of which can often lead to expanding our capacity as a school.

The action plan will require some level of documentation. This could range from an agreement contained within meeting notes or more formal documentation such as an Individualized Learning Plan (ILP)/Individualized Education Plan (IEP). Regardless of how the plan is documented it is important to include a progress monitoring schedule and method. For example, a second grade student could have an intervention plan that she will be monitored for words read per minute at an instructional level every two weeks.

**Interventions for ELLs**

In designing interventions for ELLs with learning needs, schools should use a *problem-solving approach*: a process of adapting instruction for an individual student, rather than a *standard protocol approach*: where all students with similar difficulties receive the same research based intervention (Nelson & Damico, 2006). Furthermore, Marler & Sanchez-Lopez (2006) propose six factors that influence the success of interventions for ELLs:

1. **Comprehensibility:** Is the intervention comprehensible given the ELL's level of language proficiency? Is it necessary to translate the intervention plan for the student and/or parents?

2. **Active and Authentic Engagement:** Do meaningful, interesting, and functional learning activities promote active interaction, which is essential to language acquisition and conceptual learning?

3. **Transfer of Skills and Concepts:** Does the intervention facilitate the transfer of learning from one language to another, and take into account the similarities and differences between the home and second language?

4. **Asset-Based:** Does the intervention build on linguistic and academic strengths and home language abilities?

5. **Social and Academic Language Proficiency:** Does the intervention focus on developing academic language as well as content skills and concepts?

6. **Time:** Does the intervention take into account the typical length of time required to develop the academic English language proficiency required to manage general education classroom instruction? Consistent research has shown that this may be as long as five to seven years (Goldenberg, 2013).

When designing an intervention plan for a multi-lingual student who has both language and learning goals, some key principles need consideration:

> *Comprehensive data collation and assessment suggests that Casey, the student described in the vignette at the beginning of this section, has a diagnostic profile of a Specific Learning Disorder with an impairment in reading. The recommendation from the psychoeducational evaluation indicates interventions to build phonological processing, knowledge, and application through a multi-sensory approach. In addition, ongoing EAL support is required to foster Casey's English language proficiency. Instruction to support the development of written communication in L1 also needs to be documented in a cohesive learning plan. As Casey's World Language is his L1, collaboration with the World Language teacher and his parents is required.*

- ***Co-development of an Individualized Learning Plan*** is required to ensure measurable goals in both language acquisition and the specific targeted area for learning. The development of this plan is the shared responsibility of all stakeholders (e.g. EAL and Learning Support teachers, classroom teacher, parents, and student).

- *A **support or case manager overseeing the implementation***, monitoring, and review of the ILP needs to be determined. This person is typically but not always the Learning Support specialist.

- *A **variety of instructional strategies***, in addition to goals, are incorporated into the plan. Service delivery options are decided by stakeholders and reflect the needs of an individual student. Support from both EAL and Learning Support teachers may be needed. A communication system for ongoing observational notes by all teachers is agreed upon (e.g. Google Docs, Evernote). In addition, a collaborative planning time for teachers to meet each week/cycle is determined to support the co-planning, co-teaching, co-assessing, and co-reflecting process of teaching and learning.

- ***Differentiated assessment:*** *Ongoing formative assessment* provides real-time learning data to inform instructional content and strategies, through hinge-questions and feedback that helps to move the learner forward. On the other hand, standards-based and performance-based summative *assessment of learning* can be useful if it is differentiated to build on student assets, and outcomes can be shared at ILP/IEP review meetings.

- ***Asset-based interventions*** should be culturally and linguistically relevant and promote active and authentic engagement.

- ***Maintain optimism and high standards*** when supporting the learner, acknowledging the student's efforts and the processes involved in learning.

- ***Metacognition*** should be promoted for all students. All adults should be intentional about developing each child's metacognitive awareness of his/her own learning and supporting the child in enhancing a knowledge of self as learner.

---

Key Ideas:
- ELLs typically take five to seven years or longer to acquire the academic English skills needed to thrive in a regular classroom (Goldenberg 2013). Learning English while learning in English is double the work.
- There are well established markers for distinguishing typical development from a possible learning disability (see table - Similarities Between Language Acquisition and Learning Disabilities).
- It is critical to gather descriptive data in English and L1 in order to apply accurate interventions.

## PART IV: DEVELOPING PROFESSIONAL CAPACITY

*"My dear, here we must run as fast as we can, just to stay in place. And if you wish to go anywhere, you must run twice as fast as that."*

*The Queen, Alice in Wonderland*

---

**Philip's big words:**

*Judith Henry was puzzled by a student in her first year Higher Level Psychology class. Although Philip was a charming and gregarious young man with very good social skills, she noticed that his writing seemed repetitive and simplistic. In oral interactions, Philip seemed to understand the essay questions she assigned; however, his written responses never addressed the heart of a question directly; content and complex thought were only minimally represented, and Judith had to look hard to identify it. In fact, Philip's essays were often laced with the "big words" or content specific vocabulary of the unit, but not used in a way that indicated understanding or meaning. Moreover, Philip didn't seem to understand the demands of specific cognitive processes required to answer essay questions. For example, he was unsure of how to "analyze", "compare", or respond to questions that began with "discuss".*

*Philip's school records indicated that, while never a stellar student, he had made it through his courses without being noticed for academic needs. He had never been referred for Learning Support. Philip's school records were peppered with teacher comments such as, "Philip is a great kid -- You need to work on your writing", indicating that previous teachers had picked up on writing as a specific area of challenge, but not worried about it enough to be referred for support. And now Philip was in the first year of the IB Diploma Program.*

*In conversations with Philip, Judith came to learn that Philip could speak many languages with ease. Having been born in Greece, his family had moved to the Philippines and then to Hong Kong before arriving in Malaysia. Philip had attended international schools all his life and English was his sole academic language. While the language of the family was Greek, Philip was able to converse in Tagalog and Cantonese with different friends in his class. Clearly, Philip's social skills and charm has carried him through school. Judith was very cognizant that this would not be enough to get him through the Diploma Program.*

*Judith wondered, "What do I need to do in order to serve Philip well? What will he need in order to succeed at the Diploma?"*

**A New Approach is Needed** (Who we were is no longer enough)

While students like Philip are not new to international schools, there is increasing recognition of this population of children who appear to have complex linguistic needs for academic success. With globalization, students like Philip are part of a growing population appearing in international schools.

In Philip's case, he needed support to develop the linguistic building blocks necessary for abstract, conceptual development and reasoning. Since Philip had attended international schools all his life, he technically didn't qualify as an ELL student. He had also never been referred for Learning Support, yet clearly, he needed some kind of help. Who should be responsible for this?

Educators are gradually becoming aware that the learning needs of children like Philip can't be met by the neat EAL/Learning Support departmental structures, and that something different, a new approach, is needed. Previously, Diploma teachers like Judith could see themselves simply as content area specialists whose job it was to deliver content. Content delivery is no longer enough to ensure student success in school. A new perception of self, a more complex identity is needed.

**Today's Teachers** (Who do we need to be?)

Teachers in today's international schools need to be resourceful in the face of new and complex learning challenges appearing in students. And they need to develop a willingness to serve all students in their classes, not just the ones who might be easily reached.

The principal attribute of such teachers is to be self-directed individuals who don't need to be reminded of their responsibilities in serving students. We want teachers who are able to self-manage, self-monitor, and self-modify (Costa & Garmston, 2015). Like Judith, we want teachers who recognize they play key roles in the individual successes of students, and who strive to meet that challenge.

***Self-Directed and Emotionally Sensitive:*** Such teachers are emotionally intelligent individuals who are able to develop strong and positive learning relationships with students. Research from the 1990s into the attributes of teachers most likely to increase student commitment to learning provides us with the following list of characteristics. Students want teachers who:

- Enjoy teaching the subject
- Enjoy teaching students
- Make the lessons interesting and link them to life outside school
- Will have a laugh but know how to keep order
- Are fair
- Are easy for students to talk to
- Don't shout
- Don't go on and on about things (e.g. how much better other classes are or how much better an older brother or sister was)
- Explain things students don't understand without making them feel small
- Don't give up on students (Rudduck, Day & Wallace, 1997, p. 86)

Interestingly, most of the list of attributes focuses on teacher relationships with students, indicating the crucial importance of emotional intelligence. Being deliberate about developing positive relationships for learning is a key attribute.

When teachers are asked, "How important is it for your students to like you?" many teachers respond by saying, "This isn't a popularity contest. I don't need to be liked, but I do need to be respected." When the same question is posed to students or parents, that is, "How important is it for your teacher to like you?" the answer is different. Parents and students alike say, "It's crucial."

### Nice is Not Enough

While high degrees of emotional intelligence are crucial, EQ by itself is not enough. Self-directed teachers also need to be passionate about what they teach, knowledgeable in their areas of specialization, and "make the lessons interesting and link them to life outside schools." Like adults, students seek relevance and meaning in the work they do.

*Collaborate AND walk on water!:* Self-directed teachers will know when they need help and know which colleagues to seek help from. They will develop the skills, including communication skills, necessary for successful collaboration and understand the strength that comes from working in teams.

*Giving adults permission to learn:* One of the seldom articulated assumptions held by some teachers is that an adult who needs to learn will be perceived by others (especially those in authority) as an individual with professional weaknesses or deficits. For example, few prospective teachers view job selection interviews as opportunities to explicate their areas that require growth.

Adult learning and the exploration of deeply held assumptions is a risky business and will only happen when there is a pervading culture of relational trust. Relational trust is forged upon clearly understood obligations of self and clearly understood expectations of others. In other words: I know what I am obliged to provide to others and I know clearly what I can expect from others. Bryk and Schneider (2003) identify four criteria for discernment (characteristics that make people trustworthy): respect, personal regard, competence, and integrity.

Relational trust is about recognizing our dependence on others and decreasing the anxiety that often accompanies that sense of vulnerability. School leaders are critically important in creating a culture of relational trust in which adults will come to believe that they have the permission to learn, to question and challenge previously held assumptions and mental models, and re-invent themselves professionally. The most effective school leaders do this by engaging in public learning. We hear this in meetings when the principal announces, "I don't think I believe that any more." Or the head of department comments that she "is rethinking that notion."

## Leaders of Adult Learning

In the past, EAL and Learning Support teachers considered themselves to be teachers of students. This may have worked well at a time when we perceived learning challenges to be simpler than they are now, when we believed in "pure types" and when children's needs fell neatly into the "EAL" or "Learning Support" boxes. This is no longer the case. Especially true in our international schools, we should expect increasingly diverse and complex learning challenges in our students.

As such, it is no longer sufficient for EAL and Learning Support teachers to consider themselves solely as teachers of children, and they need to develop their identities as leaders of adult learning (Kusuma-Powell & Powell, 2015). Their service as coaches in the ongoing learning of teachers is now critical. We need leaders amongst the teaching staff who will support adult learning about ELLs, diverse learners, language acquisition, and about the process of learning itself.

## A New, More Nimble Identity

Because it is impossible to predict when, where, or how learning challenges will occur in the learning cycle, teachers today need to be nimble, flexible, and resourceful in order to meet these challenges. In schools of the past, structures were developed to support the adult management of learning. These structures were often convenient for adults, and not necessarily thoughtful about the needs of students. As such, we have heard stories of students locked away in EAL or Learning Support programs for years, receiving "support" in outdated, ineffective ways. This is the opposite of being nimble. With respect to learners and their needs, today's nimble teacher is:

- sensitive
- proactive
- responsive
- efficacious
- agile
- empathic

## Values and Principles that Guide Professional Learning

Teachers in international schools have a unique opportunity to learn from one another given opportunities for flexibility and the wealth of diverse perspectives and expertise in our schools. We can and must break down the "silos" in which we have traditionally taught in order for our students and ourselves to thrive. To grow, we need to develop as leaders of all learners in our schools. By working in collaborative teams, and learning from each other, we are better prepared to meet the complex needs of our ELLs with learning differences.

***Leading adult learning and improving collaboration:*** Dilts (2003) has noted that, in order to affect learning at one level, we need to pitch adult learning outcomes at least one level above. The lower levels of Dilts' framework (environment, behaviors, capabilities) engage learning at technical levels whereas the upper reaches (beliefs, values, identity, and mission) focus on transformative learning (Powell & Kusuma-Powell, 2013). Knowing this gives us an indication that it is necessary to provide each teacher with appropriate supports and challenges.

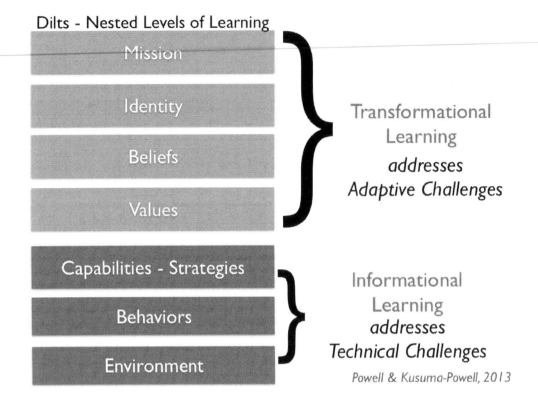

Dilts - Nested Levels of Learning

Mission

Identity

Beliefs

Values

Transformational
Learning
*addresses*
*Adaptive Challenges*

Capabilities - Strategies

Behaviors

Environment

Informational
Learning
*addresses*
*Technical Challenges*

*Powell & Kusuma-Powell, 2013*

Dilts' framework provides a structure or model for adult professional learning. Adult professional learning rarely transfers into enhanced classroom instruction unless it is pitched at the level of values, beliefs, and identity. Having said that, environment, behaviors, capabilities, and strategies are also essential features of professional learning.

As we transition from defining ourselves as either an EAL or Learning Support specialist to a facilitator of learning for culturally and linguistically diverse learners, we need to be aware and explore our beliefs and values. As our values and principles become increasingly clear, we may find the form of our service delivery will change.

While schools will have specific mission and vision statements and annual school-wide professional development goals, the most effective adult learning initiatives involve considerable teacher self-direction and autonomy. Teachers need to be self-managing, self-monitoring, and self-modifying. They need to be the architects of their own learning because only then will that learning transfer to improved practice in the classroom. In other words, within the school's guidelines and priorities established for professional development, the teacher plays a key role in determining the areas in which they need and/or wish to develop.

Given that we can expect a certain proportion of the student population to be in need of both EAL and Learning Support, it is desirable that the service providers be knowledgeable and skilled in both areas. This does not suggest that we don't need highly skilled and experienced specialists, rather that a more integrated approach to professional learning may be appropriate. This nimble new identity is most supportive of Tiers 1 and 2, while Tier 3 still requires specific Learning Support and EAL specialist expertise.

## Necessary Knowledge and Skills

*The Learning Process:* It goes without saying that teachers need to have an overarching understanding of how learning takes place. This might include a knowledge of working memory, how students construct meaning based upon prior learning, how different kinds of attention can be used in the classroom, and what structures might be used to support student reflection and metacognition.

*L1 and additional language acquisition and development:* Teachers also need to be aware of the similarities and differences between L1 and additional language acquisition and development. As international schools develop RTI structures, all teachers should familiarize themselves with interventions that are effective with both ELLs and students with learning disabilities. A clear understanding of a reasonable trajectory for student language acquisition and progress will also allow teachers to identify students who are not achieving expected benchmarks. Finally, developing compassion and understanding for those children whose L1 alphabet is other than Latin will help us to recognize that these students will need to learn and be taught basic literacy and phonics skills in English. This creates a cultural learning gap while students learn to "read and write again" and should not be confused with learning differences which may have a neurological basis.

## Interfering Variables and Cultural Sensitivity

Also of importance, is an awareness and sensitivity to issues beyond learning English and learning disabilities that may inhibit student learning. We refer to these as interfering variables. While international schools tend to cater to affluent families with professional backgrounds, we nevertheless encounter children who have experienced the traumas of war, persecution, and cultural displacement.

Today, we are seeing millions of refugees fleeing their homelands. Many of these individuals do not fit traditional schemas of the impoverished refugee. A considerable number of these refugees are educated middle class citizens who may want an international school education for their children. These youngsters will come to our schools with specific psychological needs to which we need to be sensitive. Educators need to be mindful that there may be other interfering variables that account for a student's lack of progress beyond a simple identification category of EAL or Learning Support.

Teachers also need to be sensitive to interruptions, gaps, or differing national systems, and cultural norms in a student's formal schooling. One example:

> *Fatima completed all of her primary education at an international school in Europe before her family was transferred back to their home in Yemen. Once in Sanaa, cultural forces conspired to depreciate the importance of education for girls, and Fatima did not attend school for two and a half years. During this time, the focus was on arranging a suitable marriage for her. Thus, Fatima missed almost all of middle school. At the age of 13, the father was again transferred to an international setting and Fatima was enrolled at an international school in ninth grade but had missed all of the foundational work of middle school. Teachers need to be sensitive to the fact that there can be forces far beyond the control of the student or even parent that can interfere with student progress and achievement.*

Our professional identity has shifted in the last 20 years. We have seen two major developments in international education that have been game changers for teachers and schools. First is globalization and the movement of families from country to country for employment and economic reasons. Second is the plethora of research on how the brain actually learns. We have learned more about how the brain works in the last two decades than in all of the rest of human history combined. These two factors make education one of the most complex professions. As a result, teachers need to learn how to learn from each other. They need to learn the specific skills of collaboration and coaching -- neither of which comes naturally to most of us. It is no longer sensible, fair, or effective to ask teachers to fly solo.

Key Ideas:

- A new more nimble teacher identity is needed to address the learning challenges of students learning English *and* experiencing learning difficulties.
- It is no longer sufficient for EAL and Learning Support teachers to consider themselves solely as teachers of the students "identified" within siloed departments.
- Core understandings about learning and language acquisition are the responsibility of all teachers.
- Teachers need to reconsider their roles and take up the challenge of becoming leaders of adult learning.

## PART V: CONCLUSION

One of our greatest challenges in international schools is the effective inclusion of diverse learners. When learning differences are accompanied with matters of English language acquisition, the challenge can become even more complex and the need for meaningful adult learning becomes even more important. The legacy of historical isolation in international schools coupled with assumptions about learning that lead to a false dichotomy necessitate creating the conditions in schools where we learn how to learn from each other and perhaps more importantly, from our students.

There is no doubt that teaching is multifaceted, made even more so by the richness of our diverse, international school populations. As professional educators, we hold high standards for ourselves and our students and as such can feel the pressure in trying to meet all needs at once. While we encourage international schools to become more inclusive of students learning English and those with learning challenges, we realize this change does not happen overnight. No worthwhile transformation does. Transformation starts by doing *something*, even if it seems a small step in an inclusive, truly collaborative multidisciplinary direction. One small step, and then another, is better than waiting until the "perfect" fully developed plan is in place. One person, or a few, can act as a catalyst for the transformation.

Therefore, if you can do just a few things right now to begin your transformation, we wish to inspire you to:

- Meet regularly in Student Support Teams that include both EAL and Learning Support specialists to have structured conversations about students, while exploring your collaboration and ways forward.
- Next time your team discusses an ELL that is not learning along a typical pathway, ask "What supports does this student need in order to learn?" rather than "Which program - EAL or Learning Support - should provide the service?" Commit to putting students, rather than labels, at the center of the conversation.
- First inquire whether the instructional environment is sufficiently differentiated and accessible, before trying to determine if a student has a learning difference.
- Examine how students' home languages can be used as assets, for opening a window into unique learning pathways, as a tool for supporting academic achievement, and as a bridge for engaging parents as essential partners in the learning process.

- Find an article on best practices in EAL or learning disabilities and share it with colleagues, setting a date to discuss new learning; launch the collaborative conversation.
- Share this document amongst your leadership team, Learning Support, and EAL colleagues and have a conversation about the ideas presented.

## Bibliography and Suggestions for Further Reading

Adelson, V. Geva, E. & Fraser, C. (2014). *Identification, Assessment, and Instruction of English Language Learners with Learning Difficulties in the Elementary and Intermediate Grades.* A guide for educators in Ontario school boards, March 2014.

Barth, R. (2006). *Improving Relationships Within the Schoolhouse.* Educational Leadership, Vol. 63, No. 6, March 2006.

Bryk, A. & Schneider, B. (2003). *Trust in Schools: A Core Resource for School Reform.* Creating Caring Schools, Vol. 60, No. 6, pp. 40-45, March 2003.

"Center on Response to Intervention" *www.rti4success.org.* American Institutes for Research, 2007-2012.

Chiappe, P., Siegel, L., & Wade-Woolley, L. (2002). Linguistic diversity and the development of reading skills: A longitudinal study. *Scientific Studies of Reading*, 6, 369-400.

Christo, C., Sibert, M., & Borisov, N. (2013). *Identifying English Language Learners with Dyslexia.* Mini-skills workshop presented at National Association of Schools Psychologists Convention, February 2013.

Cloud, N. (2006) Bilingual education practices. In G.B. Esquivel, E.C. Lopez & Sara Nahari (Eds) *Handbook of multicultural school psychology.* Hillsdale, NJ: Lawrence Erlbaum Associates, Inc.

Cloud, N. (2012). *How can we best serve English language learners who do have special needs, such as a disability?* In E. Hamayan & R. Freeman Field (Eds.) English language learners at school: A guide for administrators, 2nd ed. Philadelphia: Caslon.

Costa, A. & Garmston, R. (2015). *Cognitive coaching: Developing self-directed leaders and learners, 3$^{rd}$ Edition.* Lanham, MD: Rowman & Littlefield.

DeBarger, A. H., Penuel, W. R., Moorthy, S., Beauvineau, Y, & Harris, C. (2011). *Formative assessment practices to promote model-based reasoning in Earth science.* Paper presented at the Annual Meeting of the American Educational Research Association, New Orleans, LA.

Dilts, R. (2003). *From coach to awakener.* Capitola, CA: Meta Publications.

Echevarria, J. and Hasbrouck, J. (2009). *Response to Intervention and English Learners.* CREATE Brief. Washington, DC: Center for Applied Linguistics.

Gaviria, A. & Tipton, T. (2012). CEP-EL *A Comprehensive Evaluation Process for English Language Learners: A Process Manual.* San Diego Unified School District 2012.

Genesee, F., Paradis, J., & Crago, M. B. (2004). *Dual language development and disorders: A handbook on bilingualism and second language learning.* Baltimore, MD: Paul H. Brookes.

Gersten, R. & Geva, E. (2003). *Teaching Reading to Early Language Learners.* Educational Leadership, Vol. 60, No. 7, pp. 44-49, April 2003.

Goldenberg, C. (2013). Unlocking the Research on English Language Learners. *American Educator.* Vol. 37, No. 2, Summer 2013.

Gottlieb, M. (2013). *Essential Actions: A Handbook for Implementing WIDA's Framework for English Language Development Standards.* Board of Regents of the University of Wisconsin System, on behalf of the WIDA Consortium. www.wida.us

Gray, B. (1989). *Collaborating: Finding Common Ground for Multiparty Problems .* San Francisco: Jossey-Bass.

Healy, K., Vanderwood, M. & Edelston, D. (2005). *Early Literacy Interventions for English Language Learners: Support for an RTI Model.* The California School Psychologist. Vol. 10, pp. 55-63, 2005.

Hill, J. & Flynn, K. (2006). *Classroom Instruction that Works with English Language Learners.* Association for Supervision and Curriculum Development (August 2006).

Klingner, J. & Eppolito, A. (2014). *English Language Learners: Differentiating Between Language Acquisition and Learning Disabilities.* Council for Exceptional Children, January 2014.

Kusuma-Powell, O. & Powell, W. (2015). 'Raising the status of learning support teachers,' *Educational Leadership, 73(4),* 62 - 67.

Lesaux, N. & Siegal, L. (2003). *The Development of Reading in Children Who Speak English as a Second Language.* Developmental Psychology, Vol. 39 (6), Nov. 2003.

Marler, B. & Sanchez-Lopez, C. (2006, April). *Distinguishing learning disabilities from academic difficulties for English language learners.* Retrieved Presentation at the 2006 Council for Exceptional Children's Conference. Salt Lake City, Utah.

Meyer, A. & Rose, D. & Gordon, D. (2016). *Universal Design for Learning: Theory and Practice, 1st Edition.* CAST Professional Publishing an Imprint of CAST Inc.

Nelson, R. & Damico, J. (2006) Qualitative research in literacy acquisition: a framework for investigating reading in children with language impairment. *Clinical Linguistics & Phonetics.* Volume 20, Issue 7-8, (2006) Sep-Oct; 20 (7-8):631-9.

Nordmeyer, J. (2008). *Delicate Balance.* Journal of Staff Development, National Staff Development Council, Vol. 29, No. 1.

Nordmeyer, J. (2010). At the Intersection of Language and Content. In *Integrating Language and Content,* Nordmeyer and Barduhn (eds.). Alexandria, VA: TESOL.

Nordmeyer, J. *(2015). Collaboration.* EARCOS Tri-Annual Journal. East Asia Council of Overseas Schools.

Paradis, J., Genesee, F., & Crago, M. (2011). *Dual language development and disorders: A handbook on bilingualism and second language learning, 2nd Edition.* Baltimore, MD: Paul H. Brooks.

Paradis J., Genesee F. & Crago M. (2014). *Dual Language Development & Disorders: A Handbook on Bilingualism & Second Language Learning, Second Edition (CLI) 2nd Edition* Paul H Brookes Pub Co.

Pelletier, K., Armitage, K., Durham, A., Hanagan, B., Nordmeyer, J., Sack, D., Small, S., Solomon-Saleem, K. & Warner-Dobrowski, C. (2015). *Processes and Tools to Support Data-Driven Decision Making in Learning Support.* CreateSpace Independent Publishing Platform.

Powell, W. & Kusuma-Powell, O. (2007). *Making the Difference: Differentiation in International Schools.*

Powell, W. & Kusuma-Powell, O. (2013) *The OIQ factor: Raising your school's organizational intelligence.* Suffolk, UK: John Catt Educational.

Rudduck, J., Day, J., & Wallace, G. (1997). 'Students' perspectives on school improvement', in Hargreaves, A. (ed) *Rethinking educational change with heart and mind,* 1997 ASCD Yearbook. Alexandria, VA: ASCD.

San Diego Unified School District (2012) CEP-EL: A Comprehensive Evaluation Process for English Learners - A Process Manual. https://www.sandiegounified.org/sites/default/files_link/district/files/dept/special_education_/ParentServices/CEP-EL%20Manual.pdf

Sanchez-Lopez, C. (2012) *How can we distinguish a language difficulty and a learning disability?* In E. Hamayan & R. Freeman Field (Eds.) English language learners at school: A guide for administrators, 2nd ed. Philadelphia: Caslon.

Short, D. and Fitzsimmons, K. (2007). *Double the Work: Challenges and Solutions to Acquiring Language and Academic Literacy for Adolescent English Language Learners.* NY: Carnegie Corporation.

Vanderwood, M. L., Tung, C., & Arellano, E. (2014). Application of a Multi-tiered Support System with English Language Learners: A Case Study Demonstration. International Journal of School and Educational Psychology, 2, 45-53

Vaughn, S., Mathes, P., Linan-Thompson, S., Cirino, P., Carlson, C., Pollard-Durodola, S., et al. (2006). Effectiveness of an English intervention for first-grade English language learners at risk for reading problems. *Elementary School Journal*, 107, 153-180.

WIDA Consortium (2013). *Developing a Culturally and Linguistically Responsive Approach to Response to Instruction & Intervention (RtI2) for English Language Learners.* Board of Regents of the University of Wisconsin System, on behalf of the WIDA Consortium. www.wida.us

WIDA Consortium (2014). *Culturally and Linguistically Responsive RtI2 Planning Form.* Board of Regents of the University of Wisconsin System, on behalf of the WIDA Consortium. www.wida.us

Wiliam, Dylan (2015). Designing Great Hinge Questions, *Ed Leadership.* September 2015, Volume 73, Number 1. Alexandria, VA: ASCD.

*Written at American School of The Hague*
*December 12-13, 2015*

*Special thanks to Danette Sack for hosting this collaborative session.*

# *Notes*

# *Notes*

# Notes

Made in the USA
Las Vegas, NV
06 April 2022